DOWN
THE
PLUGHOLE

DOWN
THE
PLUGHOLE

Joy Richardson

Illustrated by
Sue Barclay and Dee McLean

628.1 £1
Hamish Hamilton · London

The author and publishers would like to
thank Robert Gwynne B.Sc. for his help
and advice in the preparation of this book.

HAMISH HAMILTON CHILDREN'S BOOKS
Penguin Books Ltd, 27 Wrights Lane, London W8 5TZ (Publishing & Editorial)
and Harmondsworth, Middlesex, England (Distribution & Warehouse)
Viking Penguin Inc., 40 West 23rd Street, New York, New York 10010, U.S.A.
Penguin Books Australia Ltd, Ringwood, Victoria, Australia
Penguin Books Canada Ltd, 2801 John Street, Markham, Ontario, Canada L3R 1B4
Penguin Books (N.Z.) Ltd, 182–190 Wairau Road, Auckland 10, New Zealand

First published in Great Britain 1988 by
Hamish Hamilton Children's Books
Text Copyright © 1988 by Joy Richardson
Illustrations Copyright © 1988 by Sue Barclay and (activities) Dee McLean
Design by Monica Chia

British Library Cataloguing-in-Publication Data:
Richardson, Joy
Down the plughole – (Science seekers).
1. Plumbing – Great Britain – Juvenile
literature
I. Title   II. Series
696'.1'0941   TH6124
ISBN 0–241–12089–6

Printed in Belgium

CONTENTS

Basins and baths and sinks have plugs to stop the water from running down the plughole.

Plugs have rubber or plastic parts which make them fit tightly.

Some plugs sit in the plughole. Some plugs press down on top.

How many different plugs can you find in your house?

Make a Plug

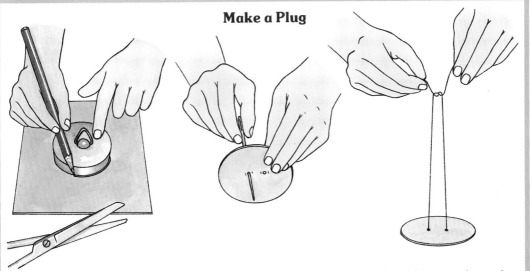

1. Draw round a plug on a piece of card and cut your circle out.

2. Make two holes in your card plug with a needle.

3. Thread cotton through the holes and tie the ends together.

4. Fit your plug into the plughole.

5. Half fill the sink or basin with water. Put your finger against the side to mark the height of the water. Count to twenty. How much water has escaped?

Try making plugs from other materials such as plastic or polystyrene.

Plugholes are not all the same.
How many different patterns
can you find?

The holes let water through.

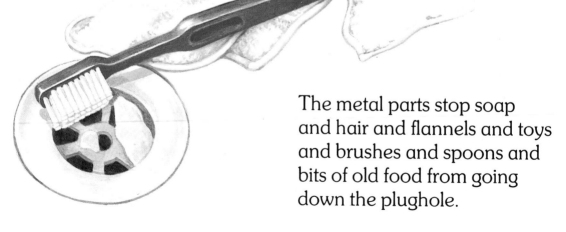

The metal parts stop soap
and hair and flannels and toys
and brushes and spoons and
bits of old food from going
down the plughole.

Plugs are usually kept on chains to stop them getting lost.

The chain helps you to pull the plug out. Water presses the plug down. If you pull on the chain it tugs on the plug and lifts it up.

Some basins have a knob between the taps. When you lift the knob, a lever moves under the plug and pushes it up.

Sometimes if you pull the plug out quickly, you hear a pop.

A little air may be sucked up from the pipe below.

Air is lighter than water so the air comes bubbling up to the surface.

Air and Water

1. Half fill a jam jar with water and then put the lid on.

2. Turn the jar upside down. Watch the air coming to the top.

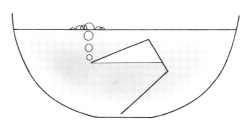

3. Turn an empty jar or plastic carton upside down. Press it down into a basin of water.

4. Turn it on its side underwater to let the air out. Watch what happens to the air.

When you pull the plug out, the water starts to run away. If you put the palm of your hand over the plughole, you can feel the water being pulled into the hole.

At first, the top of the water stays still. When it is sucked down it swirls round the hole like a whirlpool. It makes a funny sucking noise.

Round and Round the Plughole

1. Fill a sink or a basin with water. Sprinkle powder on the surface.

2. Pull the plug out gently. Watch the powder moving as the water runs away.

3. Which way did the water flow round the plughole? Did it go clockwise (like the hands of a clock) or anti-clockwise (the other way round)?

Try this experiment in other sinks and basins. Does the water always flow the same way round?

Bits of soap and dirt float on top of the water. When the water runs away slowly, a ring of scum is left behind.

It is like the tideline on a beach.

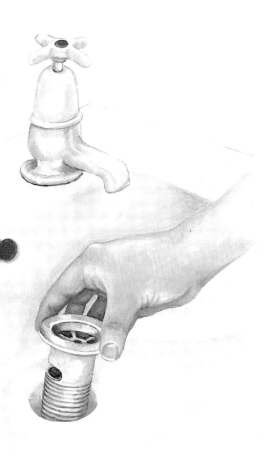

The plughole is part of a short metal pipe called the waste outlet.

The waste outlet fits through a hole in the basin.

Underneath the basin, there is a large nut on the waste outlet. The nut is screwed up tightly to hold the plughole firmly in place.

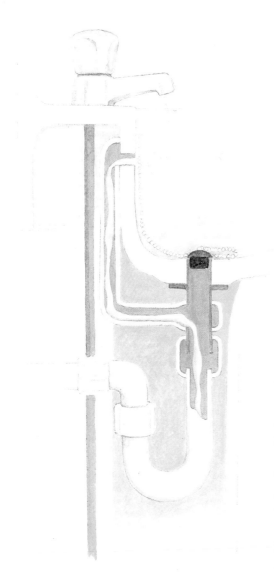

If a basin gets too full, water escapes through the overflow hole. The water runs down a pipe or channel behind the basin. It goes straight into the waste outlet under the plughole.

Some overflow pipes stick out through the wall. The water splashes onto the ground.

The overflow hole is not usually as big as the plughole.

If the plug is in and the taps are left on, there may be too much water to escape through the overflow.

The water goes on rising until it floods over the top.

Below the plughole there is a bent piece of pipe called a trap.

The trap is shaped so that it always stays full of water.

The water in the trap blocks off smelly air from the drains The trap stops smells from coming up into the room.

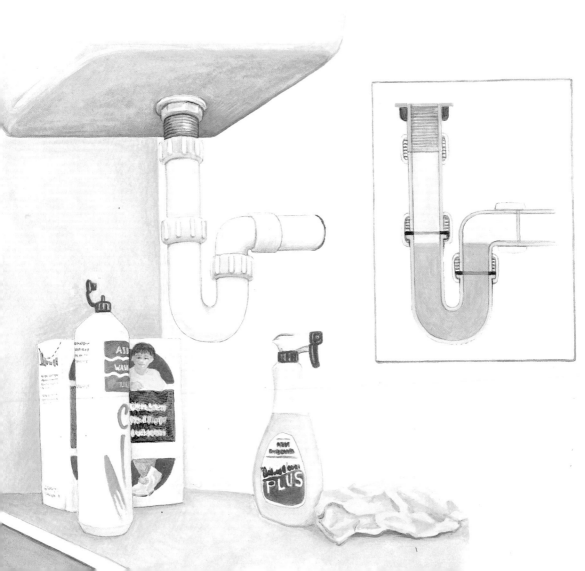

Trap

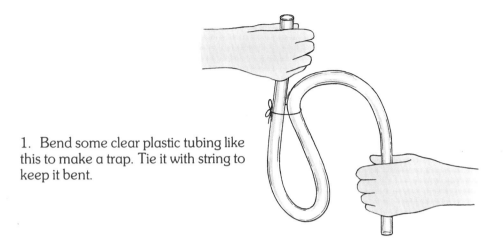

1. Bend some clear plastic tubing like this to make a trap. Tie it with string to keep it bent.

2. In a sink, run water into the top of the tube and watch it come out at the bottom. Turn the tap off and see how water stays caught in the trap.

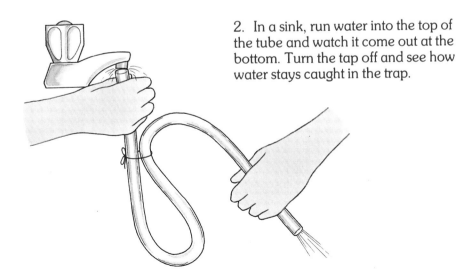

Old food and fat can block the pipe under the sink.
Water stays in the sink because it cannot run away.

A plunger like this may help to suck the blockage up out of the pipe.

You push it down hard over the plughole like a rubber sucker. When you pull it up, it sucks the blockage up out of the pipe.

If the pipe is still blocked, the trap can be unscrewed and cleared out.

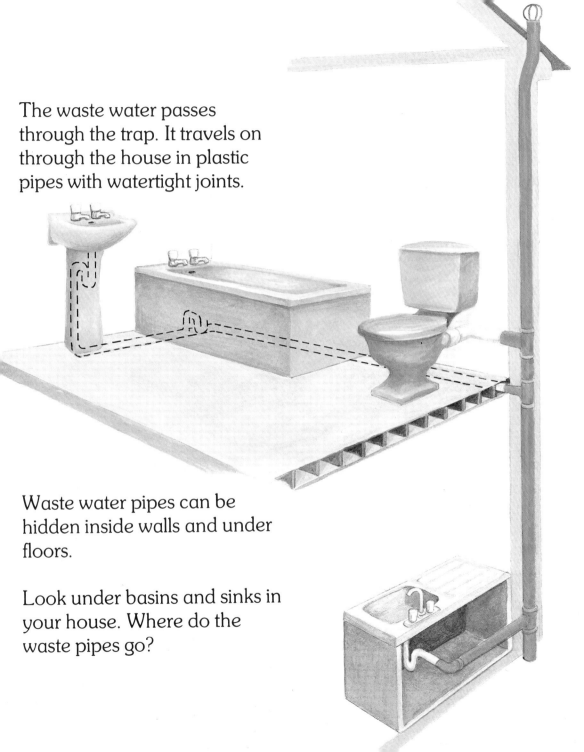

The waste water passes through the trap. It travels on through the house in plastic pipes with watertight joints.

Waste water pipes can be hidden inside walls and under floors.

Look under basins and sinks in your house. Where do the waste pipes go?

Pipes from baths and basins and sinks join up into a large waste pipe about ten centimetres wide.

In modern houses this pipe goes down inside the house. In older houses it runs down the outside. It takes the water down into a drain in the ground.

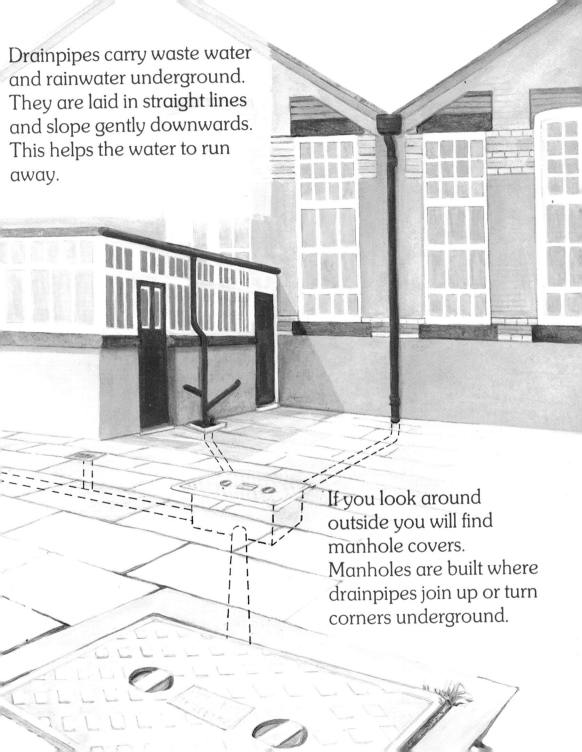

Drainpipes carry waste water and rainwater underground. They are laid in straight lines and slope gently downwards. This helps the water to run away.

If you look around outside you will find manhole covers. Manholes are built where drainpipes join up or turn corners underground.

The waste water flows through manholes as it travels away from the house.

Manholes are like boxes in the ground. The heavy covers stop people falling in.

Manholes make it possible to look at the drains without digging up the ground.

24

Sometimes drains get
blocked.

People can open up the
manholes to work out where
the blockage is.

Then they screw special rods
together and push them along
inside the drainpipe to clear the
blockage.

The drains from each house join up with a big pipe under the road. This pipe is called a sewer.

The sewer must be big enough to carry all the water from all the houses.

At busy times of day when lots of people have baths, there is a lot of water rushing through the sewer.

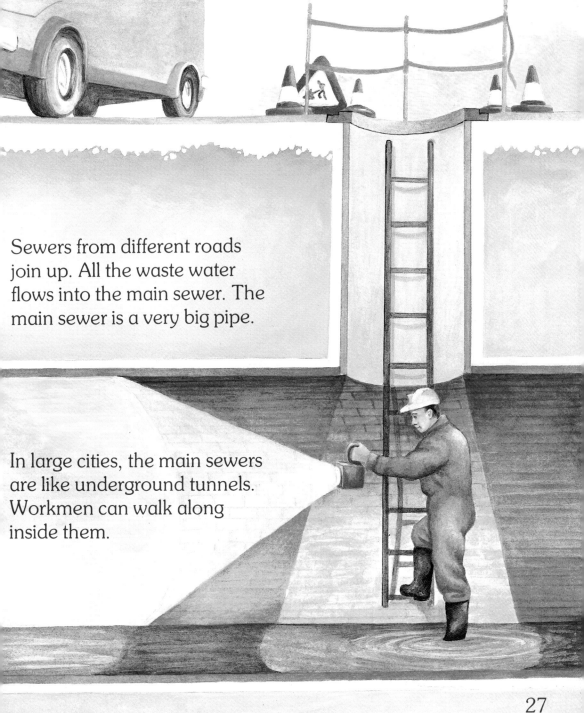

Sewers from different roads join up. All the waste water flows into the main sewer. The main sewer is a very big pipe.

In large cities, the main sewers are like underground tunnels. Workmen can walk along inside them.

27

The main sewer leads downhill to the sewage works. The waste water may have miles to travel. The journey can take several hours.

At last the dirty water flows out of the sewer into the sewage works.

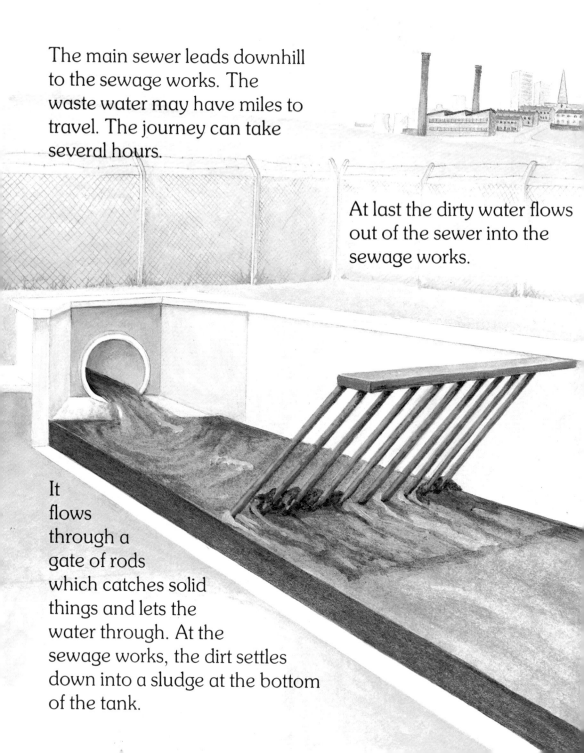

It flows through a gate of rods which catches solid things and lets the water through. At the sewage works, the dirt settles down into a sludge at the bottom of the tank.

Dirty Water

1. Put two spoonfuls of earth into a jam jar of water.

2. Put the lid on and shake the jar until the water looks dirty.

3. Leave the jam jar and look at it every quarter of an hour. What is happening to the water?

Water flows out from the top of the tank. It is then sprayed onto a bed of stones.

On the stones there are millions of tiny creatures called bacteria. They are so small you would need a microscope to see them.

The bacteria eat up any dirt left in the water.

When the water is really clean it flows out of the sewage works. It runs into streams and rivers.

The water which went down the plughole has not been wasted. If it is needed, it can be collected and used again.

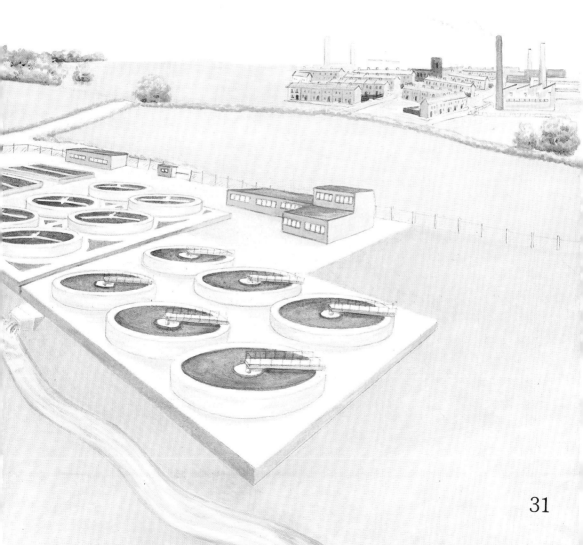

INDEX

PRINTED IN BELGIUM BY
proost
INTERNATIONAL BOOK PRODUCTION